Dear Van – You are truly an amazing man – There are few men whose entire life could be measured in heroic terms – yet you had the courage – and moral strength – and tenacity – to face the overwhelming odds of survival - most people profess to be living their faith – yet you never wavered in your chosen path – for your family. Thank you for sharing your story with me.

- Jeanne L. Noe (RN)

Dear Van – BRAVO on your book. Your life story touches the heart of every American Citizen! You overcame obstacles too great for many of us. It is an honor to have you as an American in our great country. All your friends and neighbors send you blessings forever.

- Maryruth Cutler and Laurie Russel

This book is an adventure story. It is hard to believe that someone has gone through so much. There are a lot of people out there who are still suffering. We are really blessed to live in a country like America.

- Michael Moyer

HOANG VAN...
Schooling
and
Education

A Journey from the Outside Looking In,
From Dismay to Happiness

Part Three

Hoang Van

Peppertree Press

Sarasota, Florida

…To my Father, Loi Van, for his love, his devotion to family, his dedication to the role of "Head of the Household" and his knowledge of life and survival. For teaching me all of these things and so much more.

…To my Adoptive Father, Trach Ba Vu, who opened up his home and his heart to me. For his love of learning and the strength to succeed.

…To children everywhere; "Treasure School, Grasp Education, Learn everything you can, and pass along your knowledge."

Also Available:

Hoang Van…
A STORY OF HOPE
From Dismay to Happiness

Hoang Van…
FAMILY
Commitment, Hope, and Love
From Dismay to Happiness, Part Two

Thank you my children,

Matthew Toan and Sarah Van

for all of the wonderful ways that

you will surpass me in your lives.

"Knowledge is Power"

Francis Bacon
(1561 – 1626)

Introduction

HELP WANTED: Must be able to Read and Write. (Translation: Schooling...this IS an ad in a newspaper???)

HELP WANTED: Must be able to learn from others and everyday experiences. (Translation: Education???)

HELP WANTED: Goal Orientated (Translation: A strong desire to achieve what you can do and to undertake what you don't know how to do...with as much effort as needed – Not A Question.)

HELP WANTED: Endless Commissions (Translation: Not only the dedication necessary to accomplish your immediate needs, but the rewards that come from working, wanting, and watching your children surpass you – Not A Question.)

In my first book, From Dismay to Happiness, I discussed the highlights of my life not merely for the sake of interest or astonishment but to enable the reader to get a better understanding of how my life truly did transform from one of dismay to one of happiness.

More importantly, how I was either gifted or learned the values that I treasure dearly: Family, Spiritual Guidance, and Schooling. Values, which in their very essence make me the person that I am today and the person that I hope each one of my children becomes.

My second book, <u>Family...Commitment, Hope, Love</u>, is not merely my thoughts regarding the concepts of family, but, rather, my dedication to this value and how in endless instances it was, and is, the soul of my life.

Upon completion of that book I realized that it was more important to have my third book discuss the value of schooling and let the fourth book discuss spiritual guidance as it is the value that encompasses the previous books and, essentially, made those books and those values possible.

In addition, I came to the realization that the value of "Schooling" is really not the true word I was looking for – although it seemed appropriate to me – but, rather, my concept of "Schooling" really is the combination of everything that I/we learn in a classroom as well as the overwhelming amount of knowledge we gain every single day from individuals and situations. Thus, "Education" is something that includes schooling and so much more...

"Education is the instruction of the intellect in the laws of Nature, under which name I include not merely things and their forces, but men and their ways; and the fashioning of the affections and the will into an earnest and loving desire to move in harmony with those laws."

Thomas Henry Huxley
(1825 – 1895)
A Liberal Education

…something that begins the day we are born and continues to the day we die.

"Perhaps the most valuable result of all education
Is the ability to make yourself do the thing you have to do,
When it ought to be done,
Whether you like it or not;
It is the first lesson that ought to be learned;
And however early a man's training begins,
It is probably the last lesson that he learns thoroughly."

Thomas Henry Huxley
(1825 – 1895)
Technical Education

From now on, I will do my best to separate the terms "Schooling" and "Education," however, it is impossible to say that "Schooling" is not part of "Education" while "Education" is not necessarily part of "traditional schooling."

What it all comes down to is that it is a value that has not only always been a part of my life, but a value that formed my life. No matter how smart, or stupid a man might believe he is, it is truly the individual's choice to embrace his innate knowledge and at the same time appreciate that it is just a beginning to conquer what he does not know or is not aware of in a given circumstance.

> *"Intelligence seems to be the thing that enables man to get along without education.*
>
> *Education appears to be the thing that enables man to get along without the use of his intelligence."*
>
> Albert Edward Wiggam
> (1871 – 1957)
> *The New Decalogue of Science*

So, it is pretty evident how I "value" this "value" in my life, and hopefully something that everyone feels the same way about now or they will (or at least think about) when they read this book.

The events that I discuss are things that either got me thinking and yearning for school and education but, I can honestly say that I was never aware of or would call it a "Passion" for how strong these desires were within me. Each event and each step that I was able to make, regardless of how hard – and it was hard, pushed me towards growth and, while not necessarily a plan or ultimate destination point was ever formed, the goal was always inside of me.

Nothing I say here can be considered as any sort of exact science with specific 'rights" and "wrongs". There is no reason that one person's values are definitively the values of another. I just share mine and hope that they can be a part of yours.

I am not a "teacher" in a school. There is no test at the end unless you choose to give yourself one. I do hope that you can learn from my education and expand your own. Schooling plus Education equals Learning. Learning is the foundation and subsequent levels for the growth of life.

> *"Knowledge is proud that he has learned so much;*
> *Wisdom is humble that he knows no more."*
>
> William Cowper
> (1731 – 1800)
> *That Task, Book VI, Winter Walk at Noon*

Chapter One

Unfortunately, many adults have very little recollection of their early childhoods. I say unfortunate, because in so many cases their childhood was filled with joyous moments. They might remember glimpses of a birthday party, a family outing, or momentous times in school, but alot of these memories are triggered by others' thoughts or pictures. The clarity just does not exist. However, the feelings and love from these happy times remains and helps form the character of the person they are today.

In my case, I use the word unfortunately because I remember the events all too well. Yes, what I learned during this time also formed my character but I wish the events didn't take place and I could have received my early education in a more positive set of circumstances.

Regardless, I somehow managed to prosper from what those events forced me into and changed a "Negative" into a "Positive" and utilized these negative elements to teach me things (although at the moment I had no realization of the fact) that I would treasure throughout my life.

"The direction in which Education starts a man will determine his future life."

Plato (427 – 347BC)
The Republic, Book IV

Being born in 1970 in Vietnam during a horrific war, my life began with death and destruction all around me. I can't say for certain that the horrors all around me affected me then as much as they do now. I can say for certain that they taught me something invaluable…SURVIVAL. Living while so many around you are perishing and adapting to actual bombs that were thrown in your direction – without even knowing why they were being thrown. I can't say I learned survival on my own, it was the strength of my parents that made it an innate part of my growth. There was no choice. We did what needed to do to exist and utilized any method that was available to keep our family alive. No, I didn't realize my dedication about family was being "taught" to me – for it wasn't – it was just a part of my childhood. I can't remember parties and vacations that helped make me the person I am today, I am positive the events and the early lessons that I received did.

"Adversity is sometimes hard upon a man;
But for one man who can stand prosperity,
There a hundred that will stand adversity."

Thomas Carlyle (1795 – 1881)
The Nero as Man of Letters

With the "physical" part of the war ending in 1975, my "personal war" was far worse. At the age of five, my Mother died of a horrific accident. There were no lessons that I learned from this – sorrow, tears, and loneliness aren't, in themselves, "Lessons" – yet the event forced me to educate myself in many other ways.

With my Father in psychological absence, my Brothers working, and my Sister already in a different location with a family of her own, I became the 'caregiver' and "protector" to my nine month old Brother upon my Mother's death. Yes, at the age of five I now had all of the responsibilities of a parent without a clue as to what that encompassed only that it was my "job" in the household – not a question put to me but, a definitive fact.

My Brother slept with me, I fed him, took care of him when he was ill, and watched over him twenty four hours a day, seven days a week – as a mother would watch and raise a child. Again, don't ask me how I learned to accomplish these tasks, and I definitely did not consider them lessons or, for that matter, a burden – annoyed – maybe, resentful – no. Yet, at this early age, I was given the blessing of learning the value of receiving the precious gift of taking care of another individual and raising a child. Something that has never faltered in my life.

"What we learn, we learn by doing."

Aristotle (384 – 322 BC)

During the day I carried my brother around in a "sack" on my shoulder. He was always with me, on my side or at my side while we were playing orI was cleaning him or feeding him.

With him "attached" to me, I was not able to experience the amazing joy of going to school. How a child can lay in bed and say he doesn't want to get up or he doesn't "feel good" in order not to go school is incomprehendable to me. I spent my childhood staring into a school room from the outside always yearning to be on the inside. I wanted to learn what those "symbols" on the blackboard were, I wanted to read and write, I wanted homework, I wanted to be what I consider (then and now) a "Chosen Learned Person." All of the knowledge that was in that schoolroom was not available to me and I wanted it…how in the world could anyone not want what is taught in a school? Maybe not every single thing, but definitely all of the vital basics that open doors for opportunities that one cannot fathom.

"The love of learning, the sequestered nooks,
All the sweet serenity of books."

Henry Wadsworth Longfellow
(1807 – 1882)
Morituri Salutamus

I do not regret for one single moment taking care of and raising my Brother. The bond we formed and the things that he enabled me to learn are always a part of me and there are no feelings of animosity.

However, I firmly regret not being able to attend school and receive the education the other children were getting and the marvelous things they were able to open their eyes to at an early age.

Something vital that does not need further explanation is the wonderful early knowledge I had received regarding Independence...beginning at the early age of five and vital throughout life.

Independence, Happiness and Courage come in many different forms. When you are not truly aware that you are growing up in poverty with limited food, one set of clothes per year, no electricity, etc. you learn (later maybe – at the time, you accept) you really appreciate so many small things that in today's society. No one is able to fully understand the value that they possess. In essence, while success and advancement is always on my mind, I was given the education to ignore materialism for important things such as small gifts from the heart and the love of others.

"It is not the strength but the duration of great sentiments that make great men."

James Russell Lowell
(1819 – 1891)

Love is a concept that is not taught to you. It becomes a part of you through experience, in a sense, "subliminal education." This was the case with my Father. He loved me, unconditionally and with a vast amount of support and unsaid emotion. At the time I did not realize it, but, as I got older and especially having a family of my own, I treasure this lesson that he didn't set out to teach me. It was just a part of him that became a part of me. No child can realize how hard it is for a parent to punish them – a punishment out of love to teach that what that child did was wrong.

In addition, my father also "let" me experience the importance of being a "Head of the "Household"... someone who takes responsibility for the survival and evolution of the family and its individual members.

When I was fourteen I went to work with my Father on his fishing boat. Not something I truly enjoyed or had any desire to do for the rest of my life. What that taught me was the value of the education of a trade. It doesn't matter that fishing wasn't a trade I pursued; the fact is, I learned the dedication to something new – something that is not taught in a classroom but in life experiences.

Until now, I never realized how much education I had received by the age of fourteen!

At sixteen, it was time to take my life a step further. I desperately wanted to flee the oppression of what Vietnam was encountering after the turn to Communism and find a life where freedom would lead to untold opportunities. I did not "escape" my homeland; it was time for me to graduate. At the time, graduation meant more opportunities…I never thought I would actually become a graduate.

"Only the educated are free."

Epictetus (55 – 135)

Chapter Two

In the middle of the night, at the age of sixteen, I myself, my two best friends, and twenty nine other individuals tired of tyranny and desperate to find a better life, got on a thirty two foot boat to begin our journey out of prison. Our home had become a prison, our families as precious as they were to us were inmates. We made the decision that as important as our families and our homes were, freedom was more important. The families would always be a part of us…more so when we were free and being "reborn."

"There are two great things in life,
Freedom of thought and
Freedom of action."

William Somerset Maugham
(1874 – 1915)
Of Human Bondage

Yes, we were filled with hope, optimism, faith… and, fear. Forget all of the clichés about fear and overcoming it and nothing to be afraid of, and concentrating on the future....we were scared. We knew that we could be followed by patrol boats – caught, imprisoned, or worse, we knew that we could be captured by pirates and sold to a "port" of their choice, we knew and encountered starvation and the true torments of a harsh sea. We were beyond fear of the unknowing when we were not captured. We were full of the fears of nature which were upon us. It is true that we learned lessons of survival and self preservation that could now be properly "explained" and "thankful for" – then, we were scared. Later in life, I realized one of the most important things that I incurred on that passage to freedom, something that is not a cliché; no matter how hard a challenge you must face to achieve what is right and what is an important part of your life's very being, you must face it and you can overcome it. You/I cannot give into fear – although very real – if it takes you on the path of betterment for yourself, for your family, for society.

> *"There are three lessons that I would write,*
> *Three words as with a burning pen,*
> *In tracings of eternal light upon the hearts of men.*
> *Thus, grave these lessons on thy soul,*
> *Hope, Faith and Love;*

And thou shall find
Strength when life's surges rudest roll,
Light when thou else were blind."

Johann Von Schiller
(1759 – 1805)
Hope, Faith, and Love

From the beginning of history, man has fled/ conquered hardship to work and receive opportunity. They did it, I did it, and so can you. Thus, I am not in anyway special, just proof that one can overcome an obstacle if they are willing to not only accept a challenge, but face it and come out winning.

When we finally arrived in Hong Kong, met by police, and eventually taken to an internment camp (yes, we were guarded and there were fences – but we were treated kindly, not like prisoners) a new hope and belief surpassed so many of my fears.

I received letters from my Father filled with love and letters from my Brother in the United States that he was working as quickly as possible to sponsor me to achieve my dreams…even if I did not know exactly what they all were, I knew the overall dream. To those who say, "Stop being silly, those are just dreams" I say, "A dream can't come true, if you do not have one."

While in the camp I was still faced with a harsh reality, while other children were in school learning, I spent my days wandering around the camp…how could I learn in school? I still could not read. This sounds pretty irrational, but somehow I knew I would eventually be on the other side of that window and work as hard as necessary to never again be on the outside looking in.

As I have said before, I was brought up very religiously (Catholic) and, although my beliefs were always strong, I never really thought about it much. I always recited all of my prayers because I was supposed to, and it was just a "part" of my life.

While at the camp I met a Catholic Priest who changed my life in a way that I would definitely consider a miracle. He gave me a bible. While most would say, "Big Deal" - I had no use for it since I could not read. How wrong I was! I had memorized so many prayers in the bible that I was actually able to teach myself to read by attaching the words I knew to the symbols on the page! At sixteen, I was now reading the language I was born speaking. The door had opened and I was on my way to being on the other side of the window…not in a dream, but a dream that was becoming a reality. I was going to be like everyone else; I was reading and going to go to school. I guess, not really like everyone else, I don't think most people treasure what school has to offer them. What seems like so much effort at the time, is so little effort compared to the knowledge gained and a lifetime of opportunities!

"The better part of every man's education,
Is that which he gives himself."

James Russell Lowell
(1819 – 1827)

After nine months in the camp, my papers were all completed and I was on my way to the United States. I did not know what opportunities that I would have, or what challenges were going to be set upon me, but I knew I could achieve my desires and my desires would grow with each step I took…as a man who could read.

Do not laugh for a minute…if you could not read, you would not have any idea of what was on these pages. Do not say, "So What!" You never know what words are parts of your individual treasure map and where they will lead you.

"Change is the end result of all true learning."

Leo Buscaglia
(1924 – 1998)

Chapter Three

As the plane left the ground in Hong Kong I could not honestly describe the thoughts in my head. I was excited about the opportunities and prospects for the future. I was longing to see my Brother who I had not seen in seven years. I couldn't wait to set my feet on the ground in FREEDOM.

Those were definitely my thoughts. However, this was my first flight…I really just wanted to set my feet on the ground. What did I learn on that trip? I learned that holding onto the armrests was such a small price to pay for what I was receiving.

"Education is the ability to meet life's situations."

John G. Hibben
(1861 - 1933)

Upon landing in Los Angeles, both exhilarated and afraid, the volunteers from the Catholic Church were there to meet me as promised to guide me to my next flight. Volunteers who were dedicated to helping an individual, which might seem like such a small task to most, not to one who could not understand a new language.

At the time, I didn't really consider the devotion of these people to live up to such a minuscule promise. I also didn't realize that at the very core, they were helping another individual. It meant so much to me, it calmed me, and gave me a sense of family in a context that I couldn't accept at that time. I was very lucky and again I knew that I wanted to help other people…in any way that I could. While few will admit it, helping others truly is a twofold effect – the other person is full of appreciation and joy; you/I are also full of joy. It is in no way selfish to feel better about yourself when you help other people. It is not necessary to say, "I do it just for them." Can you honestly think of a better thing to do for yourself than doing for others?

> *"Education has for its object the formation*
> *of a character."*
>
> Herbert Spencer
> (1820 – 1903)

As I was continuing on this "short journey" from Los Angeles to Atlanta and then to my final destination in Garden City Kansas, the excitement was bursting inside of me…and, of course I was nervous.

If you think I wasn't nervous, you would be crazy. No matter how excited you might be, anyone getting started on an entirely new path is nervous...call it anticipation if you'd like...it was nerves.

The thought of the future was in me, and at the same time I could not help but think about the past. Not just family or events, but what I had missed and wanted in my life...SCHOOL. It wasn't a sense of inferiority amongst others, nor a sense of belonging; it was a feeling of inferiority within myself. I never understood all of the valuable knowledge I had gained in my short sixteen years that prepared me for life nor the education that I acquired that others did not experience. Of course I would have liked things differently, but my thirst for bettering myself had taught me so many things and created a part of me that kept me pushing forward. A desire that began early, however innately, and stayed with me until this day...I might have begun with a different education, but what I learned, I learned well...and no, I don't know why and don't care why, just do your best to keep learning whatever it is that you have the opportunity to learn and the rest will eventually come if it really is that important to you - even if you don't admit it to yourself.

"Who so neglects learning in his youth,
Loses the past and is dead for the future."

Euripides
(484 – 406 BC)

I would like to say that I took mental notes of all of my early education or even that I accepted it as education, but I didn't. As a teacher, I think my Father would have given me an "A" for my accomplishments, I didn't know I was a student…a student of life, if not the school.

"When asked what learning was the most necessary,
he said, "Not to unlearn what you have learned.""

Diogenes Laertius
(circa AD 200)
Antisthenes, 4

I landed in Garden City, Kansas and a brand new life was awaiting me, or at least my efforts, as well as my Brother. An abundance of hugs and an abundance of ambition filled that eventful day. I had no idea what would come next, but it would be good because I was going to make it good.

I had gone halfway across the world to obtain the things that I could not have in my own backyard. If things are in your own backyard, utilize them, it is easier than beginning as a complete stranger in a new land with new words. I'm not saying better, but easier.

"Travel, in the younger sort, is part of education; In the elder, a part of experience. He that travelleth into a country before he hath some entrance into the language, Goeth to school and not to travel."

Francis Bacon
(1561 – 1626)
Of Travel

I was born during a war. I grew up in a land ravaged by war and changes to its inhabitants. Personal circumstances aside, I was growing up in a land where people governed who was allowed to do what and who was able to take advantage of what should have been available to all. I am not saying I was one of the few in my country, or many other countries for that matter, to not have the advantages of basic education; unfortunately, I was one of the many.

While not an American (yet) I was now standing firmly in a country that was giving me the chance to obtain the benefits of an education and the chance of freedom and opportunities…regardless of what class I was born into or the politics of a nation I had no control over…all I had to do was work for what I wanted…and I was allowed to do so.

"The primary concern of American education today is not the "good life" in young gentlemen born to the purple. Our purpose is to cultivate in the largest number of our future citizens An appreciation of both the responsibilities and the benefits to them because they are American and free."

James Bryant Conant
(1893 – 1978)

Chapter Four

You grow up in a small village where you know every face, if not the name, of every person you pass. Street names mean nothing to you, as you know every block, every house on each corner and even different odd shaped shrubs and trees. Your neighbors are always friendly and there for you, should you need any assistance, as you are for them. You have many close friends and, although you might not like some people, no enemies. You are able to find your way home in the black of night by nothing but the moonlight and the familiar sounds under your feet. You talk freely with people and laugh when possible. You have no innate fears, physical or psychological, as you don't really know what to fear…for the moment. You do your best not to think about your future and all of the things that you desire, and do your best to be happy in your own "confined universe."

One day, you take a bus for the short thirty mile trip to visit a relative as you have done in the past. The bus is crowded and your arms and knees are bumping into the person next to you. You're thirsty, you have to go the bathroom, who cares…you know you'll be at your relative's house in only a few minutes.

The bus stops and you, along with the rest of the "cattle", slowly get off the bus. You look up and there is no one there to meet you. You take a moment to look around and are unable to recognize anything, regardless of how many times you have visited before. You are alone and have no clue where you are and what you are going to do…you have taken the wrong bus and fear takes over.

You are scared, yet something inside you makes you start walking around, noticing everything you can see, and cautiously embrace this new environment and what it might have to offer. After your initial panic subsides, you know you can get another bus home so, for the moment, you want to want to explore for a short time before you return to your familiar surroundings.

"Curiosity is one of the permanent and certain characteristics of a vigorous mind."

Samuel Johnson
(1709 – 1784)
The Rambler

That, was just a "made up story," my life is far from made up, yet, it is close to that story with important differences.

I did grow up in that small village – then the similarities stop…with the exception of intense curiosity and a desire to explore. I had traveled halfway around the world, not thirty miles and, I did not arrive at my destination to find myself alone…my Brother was there to guide me along my initial journey.

Exactly where this journey was going to take me, I had no idea. I had reached the place that I had dreamed about and I was going to find all of the opportunities that I could and take advantage of them as opposed to merely dreaming about them.

I was going to learn…first, a new language, then, a new life. I was not stupid, I knew how difficult this was going to be – I also knew how the best things in life are far from easy.

"There is no substitute for hard work."

Thomas Alva Edison
(1847 – 1931)
Life

I moved in with my Brother and his family and felt very comfortable in this strange and welcoming new land. In essence, I now had FREEDOM, I was

Holcomb High School

Yesterday is already a dream and tomorrow is only a vision,
but today, well lived, makes every yesterday a dream
of happiness and every tomorrow a vision of hope.

Class Colors: Green and Silver
Class Flower: White Rose

1991

Certificate of Award
THIS CERTIFIES THAT
HUONG VAN
Is Commended for OUTSTANDING ESL STUDENT (BIOLOGY)
Certificate of Recognition
As a testimonial of the above accomplishments is granted this award.
Given at GARDEN CITY HIGH SCHOOL
Dated May 19 19 88
Gregory A. Springston, Principal
Mike Eskitch, Instructor

Certificate of Award
THIS CERTIFIES THAT
HOANG VAN
Is Commended for ACADEMIC ACHIEVEMENT
Certificate of Recognition
As a testimonial of the above accomplishments is granted this award.
Given at GARDEN CITY HIGH SCHOOL
Dated May 19 1988
Gerald H. Nosuman, Superintendent
Gregory A. Springston, Principal

seeking knowledge, and I was going to get it…I wanted it – period – you cannot be stopped from learning if you want an education and, more importantly, it is THERE for you.

I was immediately enrolled in Garden City High School in an English as a Second Language program. I cannot speak for everyone in the class, but I could not understand a word. It took me three months to be able to communicate in English and I struggled on a daily basis to learn the basic A,B,C's and struggled nightly on all of my homework. It did not matter that I had to reread things many times to understand them…I finally did understand them. I, Hoang Van, was in school!

I could not comprehend then, and not now, why anyone, with the exception of those experiencing terrible unfortunate circumstances, would not want to go to school. How could anyone think that "goofing off" or "sleeping late" could provide any sort of education for their future? It doesn't matter whether you actually enjoy all of the hard work involved; open your eyes and see how lucky you are to have a school and all that it offers at your doorstep. How long could you possibly enjoy being on the "Outside looking In" before you realize that you were given the opportunity to learn and grow rather than stand outside in the rain?

There is an old saying that, "Education does not come easy and it is not cheap." I was in America, it was not easy – it wasn't cheap – it was free - it was there for me, and not for a single second would I "regret" skipping a day of school to go the beach...I had a lifetime to get a tan and read on the beach!

> *"It was in making education not only common to all,*
> *But in some sense compulsory to all, that the destiny of*
> *the free republics of America was practically settled."*
>
> James Russell Lowell
> (1819 – 1891)

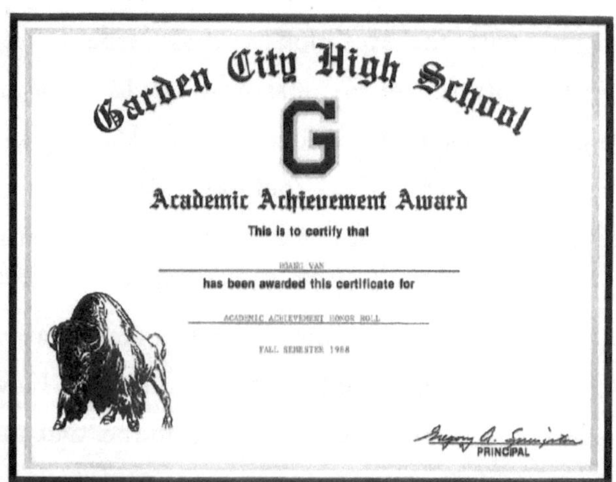

While in school, I had the privilege and honor to meet Trach Ba Vu. A man, who was not only a teacher, but a man who became my mentor and, so much more. He helped me with all of the basics of the English language and assisted me with all of my other subjects as well. He was guiding me along a path of knowledge with a friendship that went beyond school to teaching me lessons in life. A man with a family and hundreds of students who found the time to encourage me and instilled within me, the importance of hard work, caring for others, and reaping the rewards of your efforts.

> *"A teacher affects eternity;*
> *He can never tell where his influence stops."*
>
> Henry Brooks Adams
> (1838 – 1918)

After three months, my Brother was transferred to Hawaii for his job and made arrangements for me to move in with Trach Ba Vu and his family in his town of Holcomb. My studies were being continued, I had a roof over my head and the affection of an entirely new family. Do not ask me how all of this happened, but I definitely "Thank the Being" responsible. "Someone" knew how important school and education was to me, or rather, understood the importance of schooling and education to all.

After two years at Garden City High School, where Trach Ba Vu drove me every single day to school, I transferred to Holcomb High. They did not have an ESL program there and I was in the mainstream of the school. It was a much smaller school where everyone seemed to care about one another. It was hard. I was constantly challenged and, well, I had fun. All of this, with the support of Trach Ba Vu.

"Educational relations make the strongest tie."

Cecil Jon Rhodes (1853 – 1902)
Will, establishing the Rhodes Scholarship

Eventually, Trach Ba Vu became my Adoptive Father and his entire family was my Adoptive Family. Figure out for yourself what I learned from all of this (without realizing it completely at the time) and what influence it had on my values throughout my life. Figure out what, if anything, you can learn from this, regardless of where you are at the moment.

"One does not know – cannot know –
The best that is one."

James Russell Lowell
(1819 – 1891)

In 1991, after only four years in high school, I graduated with honors! I say, "only", because even though at

Holcomb
Unified School District 363
This Certifies That
Huong Van
as completed the Course of Study prescribed by the
Board of Education for the High School
and is therefore entitled to this
Diploma
Given at Holcomb, Kansas,
this twelfth day of May, 1991.

the time it seemed an eternity, four years is nothing compared to the years ahead of me – never being on "the Outside" again. I could speak, read, and write my own language…I could speak, read, and write English and all that it taught and was going to teach me. Gee, it was rough, I guess I should have given up…do I really need to finish this sentence?

> *On one occasion, Aristotle was asked how much educated men were superior to those uneducated, "As much," said he, "as the living are to the dead."*
>
> Aristotle
> (384 – 322 BC)

Chapter Five

For most of my "young life" going to school was just a "dream" for me. I always knew how desperately I wanted to go, yet I was also realistic and just kept dreaming. The thought of graduating from high school – let alone in the United States - was never thought about in my dreams – as I said, I was also realistic.

Having said that, education was so important to me that I really consider it more than a dream, it was an "obsession." In essence, for the time, it was not that I wanted to be better than anyone else, it was I wanted to be "like" everyone else. So, my philosophy on dreams… don't give up when you are determined to do something to better yourself and thus better society. Dreams really can come true…don't mislead yourself, for every dream there are alot of obstacles, hard work, and seemingly insurmountable adversities…but not unachievable.

"In every adversity to fortune, to have been happy
Is the most unhappy kind of misfortune."

Boethius
(480 – 525)

After graduating high school, where would my dreams lead me and what burning desire could I achieve next?

Every individual is born with a sort of determination for freedom and, these determinations for independence vary greatly.

Many young adults have an uncontrollable need to leave the confines of their house. I am not talking about the "lack of independence" that comes with a curfew or basic rules, but the fact that you feel suffocated in your ambitions and that your parents strictly guide every one of your actions – although in alot of cases, they are right – you still feel the need to rebel and be on your own. I feel sorry for the few who face true "oppression" from their parents…I feel sorrier for the many who think they are being "oppressed" rather than being "loved" and "taught."

Although you might (and possibly validly) consider that "imprisonment" in your home degrading, painful, and infuriating, it barely compares to the many individuals who face outside control of a far greater nature.

> *"You cannot know*
> *What you do not feel."*

Marya Mannes
(1904 – 1990)

Garden City Community College

On the recommendation of the Faculty
and by authorization of the Board of Trustees has conferred upon
Hoang Van
who has fulfilled all the requirements thereof, and is entitled to this
Associate in Science Degree
with all the honors, rights and privileges thereunto pertaining.
Given at Garden City, in the State of Kansas,
December 17, 1993.

Throughout history, there have been all kinds of tyranny, oppression, and various forms of complete denial of independence forced upon people. In my case, it was Communism. To be born in a war is horrifying enough, to grow up in a place that was supposed to be considered your "free homeland" and have your rights and free thoughts stripped away from you is unfathomable for many…understood by many more.

A country where I was not allowed to venture from my village without permission, forced to abide by laws and restrictions ranging from curfews and employment availabilities to talking, thinking, assembling, and movement. A country beset with fears of punishment, torture, slavery, and death. A country that had no need for wire fences around it…there were armed patrols either halting or deciding your every step.

I was then, and although many are still experiencing it today, not alone. But, it is not only political forces such as Communism that produce this deletion of independence. There are, and have always been, individuals forced to exist under tyrants, monarchs, dictators, and oppressors who enslave people…not merely their bodies, but their thoughts and desires. You can create your own list of the despicable entities that called, and call, themselves "leaders" from the thousands of years of humans' hardship and imprisonment, and deaths of the masses under the guise of prosperity for "all?" or, in reality, for the lives of the few.

You grow up, and grow old, being told what you can and cannot do…supposedly for the benefit of the entire nation…truthfully for the benefit of the ones in control. Opportunity seems to be a dream not worth having for it is perceived as unattainable. Many things and many people in various situations consider things unattainable. Fortunately, there are places where the only things unattainable are the things you don't work for and appreciate. Places where you can achieve your personal goals and not only thrive, but aid and empower your fellow human being…from your child to your neighbor to someone less fortunate than yourself. A place where you can complain without fear, something you should be thankful for, rather than the things you are complaining about. A place where you can be you!

In 1991, after graduating high school, I studied, passed the test, and became…

A Citizen of the United States of America.

Do not take what that stands for lightly…although in this country you are allowed to do so if that is your desire…I do not preach or judge, I just pass on my thoughts and experiences…which I am now allowed to do without persecution.

I am a person who treasures both my American citizenship and my Vietnamese heritage.

"We hold these truths to be self-evident,

That all men are created equal,

That they are endowed by their Creator

certain unalienable Rights,

That among these Rights are

Life, Liberty, and the pursuit of Happiness."

United States Declaration of Independence
(primarily written by Thomas Jefferson)
adapted by the Second Continental Congress on:
July 4th, 1776

Chapter Six

There are so many thoughts and emotions that one has, or perhaps not, when they graduate high school. For alot, it is that moment when they throw their cap up in the air and say, "Its over, I'm done, I can't wait to get out, I can't wait to be able to sleep later, what a waste of time, etc." Or, it's that moment when they get their diploma and feel, "big deal… a piece of paper for my parents…I was taught a bunch of stupid stuff."

For me, it was the exact opposite. I was not only proud of myself, but I felt like a member of a special group…a "learned group." Something that I always wanted and something that I never thought would be possible…at sixteen I couldn't even read and write my native language! Then, I learned Vietnamese, came to the United States, and learned to read and write English and graduated high school. I can definitely say to those people who threw their caps up in the air and said, "What a waste of time!" that they had no idea how valuable school and those years of education truly were…or at least to one who didn't have this "simple" advantage available to them.

Now comes the rough time for many high school graduates and yet, for some quite easy. Basically, it is the dreaded decision or, for some, a path that was already decided for them, of "what to do next." I do not mean to "belittle" the situation at all, but, for most it, comes down to (with of course some variation) the following:

- those who are happy to be out of school and don't know what they are going to do next and don't care – they are "young and free" those who either have to, by circumstance, or want to, go directly into the "job market" - not always a good career goal – definitely possible, but usually rough

- those who go to college to leave home, "party," and figure that two/four years of classes is simple enough to have those extra years of fun

- those who go to college without any true goals, desires, or direction for their future yet, they do want to learn while they are having fun

- those who want a college diploma on their resume

- those few who know what they want to study and what they want "to be" when they grow up – if a job actually decides who you "are"

 •   and then, those who want to go to college to truly learn.

They might have no idea what they want "to be" but they want to learn, experience new thoughts, and see what paths increased education will open up for them. I am not talking about the stereotypical "book-worm" but people who want knowledge. It doesn't matter 'why" or "what" the reasons are, it is just that being around people who want to learn, being around people who want to teach and being exposed to new ideas can only lead you forward – it doesn't necessarily matter where, as long as it is forward.

> *"The only thing better than education*
> *Is more education."*
>
> Agnes E. Benedict
> (1889 – 1950)

I fell into the last group. I was not smart because I went to high school - I was smart because I wanted to go to high school. I was not smart because I made the decision to go to college – I was smart because I wanted to go. I had absolutely no idea what to study, just to learn and grow. Let's face it, the more anyone knows and experiences, the more that person is prepared – and excited – about the future. I didn't decide upon my future, I just knew I wanted a future...one that would be decided (or influenced) by education.

> *"Real education must ultimately be limited to men who insist on knowing, the rest is mere sheep-herding."*
>
> Ezra Pound
> (1885 – 1972)
> *A,B,C, of Reading*

As such, I enrolled in Garden City Community College. My major was Computer Science. Yes, I laugh about that too. I had no idea why this was my major, I had no idea what I was actually learning (although I was learning,) and I was pretty positive I was not going to make Computer Science my career. Needless to say, computers are an everyday part of life – in many avenues, not just careers - and that "basic" understanding of computers I acquired is valuable just, at the time, it was rather some sort of vehicle to get through school, not a vehicle that held any specific useful purpose...other than more education, more experience, and chances to broaden my horizon. In the strictest sense, Computer Science on its own would be (and was) considered pretty useless to me, what college offered wasn't.

*"One of the benefits of a college education
Is to show the boy its little avail."*

Henry Adams
(1802 – 1872)
*(The Education of Henry Adams
– Henry Adams, John Hay, and Clarence King)*

While in college, I began volunteering for the United States Catholic Charity (USCC.) It was an "eye-opening" and wonderful experience full of meeting many caring volunteers who became life long friends and a gift of being given the opportunity to help others.

My responsibilities consisted of teaching Vietnamese individuals English, teaching them to drive, filling out paper work, and letting them know that they were not alone. I and many others were there to help them learn, get accustomed to this new environment, and cheer for them while they sincerely tried to better themselves and their families. Yes, this was a gift I received, not a job.

"Who does not befriend himself by doing good?"
Sophocles
(469 – 406 BC)
(Oedipus Colenus)

From that period on I knew, not merely felt, that I wanted to spend my life helping others. I was not sure in what capacity, but I wanted to assist others and make other people's happiness a lifelong priority.

From Vietnam, to Hong Kong, and to the United States, the Catholic Church had been such an influential force in my life. I realized that I wanted to help as many people as possible in the way that the Church had helped me. I wanted the Church and all of its "children" to be my life.

I always did, and do, treasure Schooling and always did, and do, treasure Family. I wanted the Church to be my family and give me the opportunity to help as many people as possible. I had no idea if the Church was my "true calling" however, helping people was. I made the decision to apply for Seminary School upon my graduation from college.

My life was going to thrive and change with more education, more experiences, and so much more "unpredicted growth" due to the advantages and opportunities of knowledge.

> *"Education is not a preparation for life;*
> *Education is life itself."*
>
> John Dewey
> (1859 – 1952)

Chapter Seven

In the summer of 1993, I was a High School Graduate, a Citizen of the United States, and a College Graduate! Most people would not hang these "certificates" on their walls, let alone their refrigerators, I hung them proudly around my neck.

If you didn't need to work for these things, I am happy for you. If you don't appreciate these things, I am sad for you. If you didn't learn from these things, I pity you. If you are given these wonderful opportunities, cherish them and grow from them, don't mistake their value and the influence they have on your life.

In six years I had the equivalent of fourteen years worth of schooling! I had the gift of citizenship and freedom which so many people are lucky enough to be born with and keep throughout their lives. I had "fifty" years of knowledge in my twenty three year old life!

"Time as he grows old teaches many lessons."

Aeschylus
(525 – 456 BC)

In the summer of 1993, my younger Brother was going to be married. After seven years of being physically apart from my Brother, my Father, and my homeland I was going around the world again to be at my Brother's side for this special event and at my Father's side for a love that I longed to physically feel again.

"As cold waters to a thirsty soul,

So is good news from a far country."

Proverbs 25, 25

The time on the plane gave me so much time to think about so many things, both in the "distant" past and the very recent past. In reality, while school had taught me so much, my life was far from a classic textbook scenario. I cannot say that in all of this thinking I was actually teaching myself anything. However, I learned (without actual realization) something very important.

I was going back to be with my Family and I was proud of all of the amazing accomplishments I had made and of all of the things that I had learned. Yet, it was important that I didn't go back to my family waving my successes in front of them. I was going back to "be" with them, not to be "above" them. Yes, pride within myself was important to me, but not of something to be proud.

I guess I was learning (or thinking) about the fact that to be truly "learned," you share your knowledge with people without belittling them in anyway. It wasn't necessary for me to correct people or show off to them, I needed to appreciate that what I have been able to achieve was due to their contribution, their love. I wasn't better than them, I was better Because of them. In actuality, I might have learned alot but I was not better than them. I guess it was a long plane ride filled with alot of "self analysis."

"Learning without thought is useless;
Thought without learning is dangerous."

Confucius

(551 – 479 BC)

After the plane landed in Saigon, a short stay there, followed by a bus ride, I arrived back in Lang Co. – My Home. My Father was there in the middle of the street to meet me. It is not necessary for me to describe my emotions – so valuable and so far beyond definition.

As I was hugging my Father for what seemed like hours, I knew that I was holding a man who had taught me so much. A man whose love gave me knowledge beyond any four walls. A man who gave me the courage and intense desire to achieve and better myself…not because I wanted to be better and have more than him but, because he wanted me to be better and have more than him.

"Education consists of examples and love
– nothing else."

Heinrich Pestalozzi
(1746 – 1827)

It was now time to be with my Brother. The brother who was the child I helped raise. He would never realize that he taught me more than I taught him. We both realized how much we loved one another.

Being with friends and family was an amazing experience. My Father was "showing me off" and the neighbors and relatives wanted to hear about my "adventures" and share in my knowledge of America and English. My Father was proud, I was not flashing my pride. My friends and neighbors wanted to learn from me, I was not preaching to them.

The question is, "Which came first, my thoughts on the plane or this experience?"

The wedding was an amazing and wonderful event. It is not necessary to learn something from everything in life (although we eventually do); I had fun, I was with people I loved, I was happy!

Needless to say, after two weeks of tremendous exuberance and love, it was hard to say goodbye. The hardship of leaving was far less than the joy of being there. I'm sure I don't think about that fact with everyday occurrences, I'm sure I should.

Once again, when it was time to leave I hugged my Father for "hours." Here I was holding my Father who had shared so much love and gave me knowledge of life far beyond expectation or realization.

I had been and continued to be blessed. Halfway across the world I had my Adoptive Father who also shared his love as well as his love for schooling.

Love, experience, and schooling…education. I was beyond fortunate, people – "gifts" – who made me the person I am. I thank them for the pride that I feel.

"No man can lose what he never had."

Izaak Walton
(1593 – 1683)
(*The Compleat Angler*)

Chapter Eight

Upon my return, I immediately started filling out applications for various Seminary Schools. I was ultimately accepted into Pontifical College Josephinium in Columbus, Ohio.

It is strange that one needs to apply to Seminary School. It would seem that if you wanted to dedicate yourself to Mankind, the Church, and God, you should automatically be accepted. In truth, it is for the benefit of all that there is a process of selection. If you are entering into a "profession" based on serving and helping people, you need to have the qualifications and knowledge necessary to complete such a task. The passion is definitively the most important aspect, but passion alone is not enough. In essence, you might love medicine and want to dedicate yourself to curing and healing individuals. However, if you do not have the abilities to learn the implementation and scientific foundations of your chosen profession then your passion alone will not achieve the end result. In no way does this mean that you disintegrate your passion, it means, keep your passion alive and be open to different ways (even if you do not know what they are) that you can achieve your ultimate goal of curing people. If that is your true desire, there are many avenues to take you there.

"Here the heart may give a useful lesson to the head,
And learning wiser grow without his books."

William Cowper
(1731 – 1800)
(The Task. Book VI, winter Walk at Noon)

When I entered Seminary School, I was in a state of exhilaration. Of course, I had all of the expected fears that come with living on your own, moving to a new location, beginning a new "career", etc. however, my passion to help, far out weighed my fears of the work that would be involved. I treasured the learning I was about to receive regardless of the efforts required. Like the individual dedicated to curing and healing the ill, I had made a lifelong decision. It is interesting that most consider a lifelong decision based upon their career choice rather than realizing the passion that made that choice. In addition, while I (or anyone) might make a life long commitment, one has to be open to everything else that they might want (i.e. family, travel, your individual definition of wealth, etc.) so that your passion does not fuel later regrets. No, I didn't know what all of those things were, but make sure your choice to join the "Peace Corps" won't inhibit other desires (even if you are not sure what they are) later in life. There is a balance in everything and many ways to achieve balance…for your own happiness and others. Regardless, that balance consists of learning from others and from within yourself.

> *"There are…two educations.*
> *One should teach us how to make a living*
> *And the other How to live."*

> James Truslow Adams
> (1878 – 1949)

In addition to my practical studies, the Seminary gave me the opportunity to explore many new things. I got involved in hockey and football to name but a few. I had never played these sports before or really contemplated taking time away from studies or family to enjoy such things. And I did enjoy studies and family. I guess it comes back to balance.

I had no idea, I'm not even sure if I cared all that much if I would be any good at these things. I wanted to try. Yes, sports teach alot of lessons, but that wasn't the issue. I wanted to have fun. It doesn't matter if you stop doing something intended to be fun if you are not enjoying it (I do not consider it "quitting" when you chose one recreational activity over the other) the fact is, just try…you never know where that will lead you or who you will meet.

Again, it is about fun. It doesn't matter if it is sports, the arts, or chess - enjoyment really teaches you alot without you realizing it and, if nothing else, it gives your mind and body a chance to rest from your everyday efforts and concentration – no matter how important they are to you. A balance that helps you thrive.

> *"Reading is to the mind*
> *What exercise is to the body."*
>
> Joseph Addison
> (1672 – 1719)

While the classes and schedules we kept were extremely vigorous, one of my responsibilities that I enjoyed and learned from the most was weekly pastoral work. We would spend an afternoon going out to be with people who could use comfort in one form or another.

In my case, I spent the afternoon at a nursing home. I spent time putting on shows, playing games, and providing any sort of entertainment that would provide a diversion from the mundane and make these men and women happy. It really boiled down to providing comfort and companionship…something everyone needs…something that not everyone receives.

It was an amazing experience to be able to help another person and to learn so much from them. It was an ultimate combination of education and happiness…for both of us.

I spent an enormous amount of time on my studies. They were in no way easy. I had large problems with theology and philosophy (from the "book" perspective) as my English was not strong enough to fully grasp what was required in these courses. I didn't give up. I worked hard, and in reality did not excel. Throughout, the Priests and eventually, the Bishop were concerned, yet encouraging and helpful about my performance. I would have liked to have spent more time doing pastoral work but, I needed to master these classes as well.

While I put a tremendous amount of effort into these subjects, my progression also faltered when in 1996, my Father passed away. I cannot explain the feelings to anyone who has not experienced them, imagined them or, unfortunately, not had them for the loss of a person so dear to you. In time, you come to the realization that while their death hurts you tremendously, their life was far more important. It is selfish to be engrossed with the fact that they are "gone" without appreciating the fact that they were with you. No, these thoughts did not come to me at the occurrence – if anything, the occurrence had a major impact on my well-being and my studies – but, when I was able to accept the situation, I was so grateful for my Father's love, his wisdom, and his life that the hurt of the present was far less than the joy of the past.

> *"Eternal rest, grant unto them, O Lord,*
> *And let perpetual light shine upon them.*
> *May the souls of the faithful departed*
> *Through the mercy of God rest in peace."*
>
> *"Amen"*

With my initial grieving behind me, I returned to my studies. Again, I received news from the Bishop that he was quite concerned over my lack of progress. He was in no way chastising me, he was coming to my assistance.

After further discussion with the Bishop and with his suggestion and blessing, I took my leave of absence from the Seminary. I did NOT leave the Church, just the Seminary. The Bishop helped me realize that while my passion for helping others was strong, it was more important (and realistic) to fulfill that passion in ways that would benefit myself and others in the greatest manner.

Of course at first, I felt like a failure. But in retrospect, this was definitely not the case. The Seminary increased my desire to help people and aided me in realizing that the Priesthood was not the best way for me to do so. I might have "failed" in my initial approach but I was not going to (and did not) fail with my mission.

Life does put many obstacles in our way. The thing is, they are often not obstacles but changes in our future that we are unaware of and need to accept and capitalize on. Change in course can definitely be for the better – we might not know how or why – if you never lose sight of what you want...the "hows" and "whys" will eventually come. It is hard to stay on the right path...there really is more than one path...as long as "right" is always on that path.

> *"The fact that man knows right from wrong*
> *Proves his intellectual superiority to other creatures;*
> *But the fact that he can <u>do</u> wrong*
> *Proves his <u>moral</u> inferiority*
>
> *To any creature that cannot."*

Mark Twain
(1835 – 1910)

Chapter Nine

I knew I had to take care of my younger Brother. I knew I wanted to escape the Vietnam that I was experiencing. I knew I wanted freedom and opportunity. I knew I wanted to go to school. I knew I wanted to learn to read and write Vietnamese. I knew I wanted to go to the United States. I knew I wanted to learn English. I knew I wanted to graduate high school. I knew I wanted to be an American Citizen. I knew I wanted to go to college. I knew I wanted to find a way to help people. I knew I loved my family. I knew I wanted to go to Seminary School.

Now…I didn't know what I wanted to do or where I wanted to go. I knew there had to be <u>something, somewhere</u>…but I really was at a loss for the passion I had always felt that gave me direction and purpose.

Seminary School had taught me so many things and provided so much inspiration for me that I was truly grateful for having been there. Yet, I was still faced with "Now What?" It would have been so easy to just "give up" and not care about what I was doing or where I wanted to go, however, that was not an option that I even contemplated for a moment. I was not going to ignore all that I had learned and just sit around and pity myself. I was going to take advantage of "some sort" of opportunity that was being offered to me. To be accurate, to find out what that opportunity was. My life had always been filled with enormous difficulties that somehow fueled my desire to learn and progress.

> *"Human history becomes more and more a race between education and catastrophe."*
>
> Herbert George Wells
> (1866 – 1946)
> (*The Outline of History*)

Without a definitive purpose at that point in my life, I contacted a close friend of mine who was on his way to be with his family in Buffalo, NY. I had gottten to know his family when I volunteered with the USCC and they were kind enough to invite me to join him at their home. To be truthful, I was not used to cold... you learn very quickly that Buffalo is cold.

My friend and I went on vacation to Sarasota, Florida and stayed with close friends of his parents. It was an amazing week full of joy, new experiences, water, sand, and...warmth – both inside and out.

After our return to Buffalo – and without much hesitation - the two of us decided to move to Sarasota. Yes, a quick decision and while it may have seemed like a choice out of merely wanting to leave Buffalo, it was a choice that changed the direction of my life – unknowingly and wonderfully. Thought without hesitation is not always a wise idea however, stagnation leads nowhere.

"Destiny is not a matter of chance,

It is a matter of choice.

It is not a thing to be waited for,

It is a thing to be achieved."

William Jennings Bryant
(1860 – 1925)

We were fortunate enough to move in with the family we had visited and although completely un-known to me at the time, this was a definite act of fate. Approximately three months after we arrived in Florida and had stayed with this family, the eldest daughter – who would later become my sister–in-law (fate?) – was moving with her family into a house of her own and invited me to take the extra bedroom at their house. Life was definitely forging a new direction for me with alot of new lessons…you really don't stop learning, even when you're not in school.

> *"A child educated only at the school*
> *is an uneducated child."*
>
> George Santayana
> (1863 – 1952)

A short while thereafter, my friend decided to open a nail salon while I continued to do virtually nothing – something I was not accustomed to and, believe it or not, is not really enjoyable. Go ahead, jump in a pool and do nothing but tread water. It might feel good at first when it is hot outside but after not moving anywhere, you begin to feel motionless while others around you are swimming upstream.

After he was situated, my friend suggested I should go to school (again?) to become a licensed nail technician. This was not part of any plan or desire I had ever contemplated. Yet, I enrolled, learned the profession, got my license, and joined him at work.

> *"Live as if you were to die tomorrow.*
> *learn as if you were to live forever."*
>
> Mohandas Gandhi
> (1869 – 1948)

I did not only learn the art, I loved helping people feel better about themselves, I loved the interaction with numerous new individuals, and I took every effort to learn the business aspects of the profession as well.

While I learned the technique and the aspects of the

business quite well, I would not have considered myself a "learned business man." I do not know for certain if it was things I had learned in the past or some sort of "force" within me but, I knew I was on the right path.

With the support, assurance and knowledge of friends, family, and an individual whom I had never met, I made the decision and managed to open my own nail salon. I might not have learned the intricate parts of what I was now endeavoring in my life; I had however, learned the necessity of passion and the valuable work ethics behind my choice.

"I forget what I was taught.
I only remember what I have learnt."

Patrick White
(1912 – 1990)

In 1999, the store which I still own today opened for business…not alot of business at first, but it was open. "Open" is putting it mildly; I was there all day, everyday. I loved the work, the opportunity to grow my own business, and the wonderful things that would be awaiting me from a combination of my hard work and this unexpected gift that had been presented to me for me to cherish. I did not care how hard it was going to be to "unwrap," I was going to get what was on the inside…not look at it from the outside.

"Men of genius do not excel in any profession because they labour in it,
but they labour in it because they excel."

William Hazlitt
(1778 – 1830)

I won't go into the details of all that I experienced and learned in 1999. I can say that I worked, and worked, and worked, and well, you get the idea. Somehow I just knew this business; somehow it was a miracle that would change my life in many ways…not always better on a day to day basis but, one that would definitely prove a further reward and affirmation of my decision to leave Vietnam in search of opportunity…opportunity gained by education.

"Success is to be measured not so much by the position that one has reached in life as by the obstacles which he has overcome."

Booker T. Washington
(1856 – 1915)

While 1999 was beyond difficult, I loved the work and what I could achieve. As hard as it was, the year was wonderful and a changing point in my life.

The year was wonderful until the end of the year – when another changing point occurred. One that not anyone should experience.

Chapter Ten

There are certain things in life that you do not learn from. Things that you should not experience. Things that should just not happen. Things that you are not, and never could be, prepared for. Things that you cannot explain. Things that test your beliefs. Things that later in life you can share with people in the hope that your experience and unwanted knowledge can aid them in some way. Things, that in the simplest form…are catastrophically wrong.

In December of 1999, I received a phone call from Vietnam. My brother, the child I helped raise, had died at the age of twenty four.

> *There's no tragedy in life like the death of a child. Things never get back to the way they were."*
>
> Dwight D. Eisenhower
> (1890 – 1969)

The moment I heard the words on the phone, coming from thousands of miles away, I felt lost, I felt alone. I felt anger. All of the sorrowful emotions that I felt, I will not describe. The anger was on top of the sadness and it was strong. Is it possible to be so angry at a person that you loved so dearly and is simply no longer with you? Is it possible that in some way you blame that person for leaving you, not merely the typical blame placed upon God? There is a fine line between "love" and "hate." However, in this case, I replace "hate with anger." The truth is, at least for me, there is not a fine line. The more you love someone, the more you are angry that they are no longer with you. There are many things to be thankful for, especially the fact that this loving someone was a very special gift in your life regardless of how long you are able to physically keep that gift. Truth be told, you are not thankful for the time you had, only angry at the time you didn't have.

Over time, yes it can and does happen, the anger diminishes and the love grows stronger. You thank God for the blessing of that person's life and what that person meant to you, not the anger felt because God took that person from you. The impact a person had on your life is meaningless if all you can retain is anger. Love is stronger than Anger. Love will overcome your grief. It was in no way easy. But, when you know that the person you lost loved you as much as you loved them, you go on with your life. You do not forget them.

And, they are always with you…helping you, caring for you…as you do for them.

> *"There is no cure for birth and death, save to enjoy the eternal. The dark background which death supplies brings out the tender colors of life in their purity."*

George Santayana
(1862 – 1952)

When I put down the receiver of the phone I somehow managed to put my shock and emotions on hold for a moment. There would be plenty of time for that. At that moment, I needed to take action. I was going to be at my Brother's side at his funeral. There to say "goodbye" to his <u>being</u>, not his <u>soul</u>. I did not "need" to be at his side. I did not "want" to be at his side. I was GOING to be at his side. Period. No thought, no rationale, no contemplation of not being there, not even a thought of I "had" to be there (in the sense that "had" meant it was my obligation)…it was the time to make all the arrangements necessary. This "action" was not so that I would not feel any guilt later about not going… this was for me just as much, if not more, as for him.

I honestly gave no thought to the price of an immediate airplane ticket or where that money was coming from. I gave no thought to the "dreaded" Y2K virus

that could happen on the upcoming year 2000. I was getting my ticket and I was going.

I was not going there to be angry about his death, but to be happy for his life. 'Celebration" is, of course, the wrong word, gratitude and honor are more appropriate. I was not losing him in his death. He was going to be with me in the same way that I was with him. Thousands of miles had not separated my love for my Brother. He was now going to be even closer to my heart and at my side as I was going to be at his.

> *"If we value so highly the dignity of life, how can*
> *we not also value the dignity of death.*
> *No death may be called futile."*

Yukio Mishima
(1925 – 1970)

Vietnam is a very hot country. A place where, even in 1999, very few homes had any sort of air conditioning. Yet, in the three days it took me to arrive at my Brother's side, his (my) family and friends managed to perfectly preserve his body so that I could have the honor of presiding over his funeral. It was an honor, one of not only respect, but, one of understanding of the relationship between my Brother and myself.

The ocean was such a short distance from his home. On that day, the tears made the ocean grow. Not merely tears of sorrow, but tears of gratitude. Tears that replaced the salt of the ocean with the sugar of life's sweetness.

> *"Every man dies — not every man really lives."*
>
> William Ross Wallace
> (1819 – 1881)

After only three days in Vietnam, I received a call that my shop had been broken into. It was a time for reality. It was time for me to go home to take care of my business and my future. My Brother was going with me. I often wonder if this was my Brother's way of "giving me a swift kick" and saying, "Stop mourning. Go back to growing. Take me and this experience back to your life and find a way for it to enrich both you and others. Take your sorrow and help heal others." My Brother was a very smart man.

"Wit and wisdom are born with a man."

John Selden
(1584 – 1654)

When I left Vietnam, I made a vow to both myself and my Brother's family to always be there for them and to always be in their lives. To this day, I still send my support to ensure that my Brother's children will be able to attend school and gain the advantages of education that are rightfully theirs. An education that will help them grow and achieve more than their Father ever had, as any Father wishes for his children. An education that will fill them with pride, hope, and compassion.

"A child miseducated is a child lost."

John F. Kennedy
(1917 – 1963)

As I said earlier, things do take time to accept and for feelings to change. I am no different than anyone else. The plane ride home was an eternity filled with sorrow, loneliness, and in all honesty, self pity.

I would be lying to say that the year 2000 was beginning with anything less than these tremendous emotions. Emotions which, for the time, felt like they were never going to leave me. A vacant hole in my soul that felt like it could never be filled. I was wrong. Thank you…

Chapter Eleven

I returned to my salon and found exactly what I expected. I immediately began cleaning up the utter mess, repaired what I could, and purchased the new things that had to be replaced. In essence, what a pain!

When the salon was "looking like new" I reopened and welcomed my twelve hour days. I expected to be sad, full of thought, self-pity, and a sense of loss for a long time after the funeral and the feelings did in fact, last throughout the year.

"What does not empty tomorrow of its sorrow;
It empties today of its strength."

Corrie Ten Boom
(1892 – 1983)

I look back at that sentence and realize how wrong I was during those days. I wrote that. "I expected" those emotions and I did achieve that goal. It is amazing how the mind can achieve anything that it wants once it sets a pattern of expectance. The fact is, that being continually depressed takes a lot of thought and work. When you're happy, you really do not think about the "whys" – you just are. To be depressed, you have no choice but to spend your time thinking about your situation and subsequently achieving it. I find this true in almost any circumstance…sometimes, too late. If you expect to be mournful, you will do your best to achieve it. If you expect to be happy, it just sort of happens. I am in no way saying that one should forget the realities that they are unfortunately experiencing, but change their focus, for the good of themselves and for the person you have lost.

"The reason why worry kills more people than work
Is that more people worry than work."

Robert Frost
(1874 – 1963)

So, I worked through the year. I spent all of my time trying to build my business and all of my time in a vacuum of despair. I was able to hide my emotions from customers but, when I was alone, they enveloped me. For the life of me, I have no answers about how one can remain positive about the future while in a state of depression. "Something" or "Someone" didn't let me give up on the future. I was responsible for the hurt of the present.

"There are few human emotions as warm,
comforting, and enveloping
As self-pity.
And nothing is more corrosive and destructive.
There is only one answer;
Turn away from it
And move on."

Dr. Megan Reik

I have no idea how to sum up the year 2000. I really just kept working and while I was working I was not consumed with emotion but rather, hope. I was alive. My Brother was not. My Brother did not want me to "be" the person I was allowing myself "to be" – he would have been angry in ways that I would not express here. So, there I was in my own personal version of human purgatory while on earth.

"The greatest glory in living lies not in never failing,
But in rising every time we fail."

Nelson Mandela
(1918 – 1993)

January, February, March, April, May, June, July, August, September, October, November…work and struggling to hide and control my emotions. I was not giving in – it wasn't really a conscious thought, it was the reality.

"Sorrow and silence are strong,
And patient endurance is godlike."

Henry Wadsworth Longfellow
(1807 – 1882)

And then came December, 2000. My life was going to begin the journey – quickly – to recovery.

My Adoptive Sister was having a family holiday reunion at her home in Washington State and invited me – insisted - that I come. I do not believe in sharing misery. It is not something that is a "joy to receive" by any person – no matter how kind and understanding they appear to react.

What I completely missed is that when one is around loved ones, it is not a question of sharing sorrow, it is receiving love and comfort from those around you. Unconditional love by family who are on your side and want to see you as the wonderful person you are, not the result of a current situation.

By sharing their love, hopes, and strength they, in fact, rejuvenated me in a sense of re-birth. December, 2000 with my family changed me back to the person I was – one full of spirit, courage, warmth, and a desire to utilize all that I had learned...for myself and hopefully others.

I was responsible for my own well being – and the walls I had put around myself; they made me realize I was not alone. The things New Years are made of… in many ways.

"Sorrow and suffering make for character if they are voluntarily borne, but not if they are imposed."

Mahatma Gandhi
(1869 – 1948)

Chapter Twelve

*"What we need for our happiness is often close
at hand, if we knew how to seek for it."*

Nathaniel Hawthorne
(1804 – 1864)

The year 2001 did, in fact, begin "new" for me. I was back to being the person I "was" and wanted to "be" – not the person I had become. I don't ask how, but I was able to conquer many obstacles in my life, acquire so much knowledge, and, even if not at the time of the event, learn from these obstacles and grow.

The death of my Brother was unavoidable yet, in hindsight, the year of complete sorrow and grief could have been diminished as opposed to overwhelming. It was not a case of diminishing my love or grief, but my self-pity. Don't get me wrong, I am not saying that I, or anyone, could have put aside the situation, just possibly encountered it differently. At any rate, thanks to the wonderful uplifting end of 2000, I was back. I was a person who was no longer going to hide in the past, but relish in the present and the future.

In my salon, I returned to my twelve hour days, but happily – not in avoidance. I loved what I was doing and loved the future it could bring me. I was enjoying meeting many new people and not only seeing my clientele increase, but my friendships. It sounds strange, but I was "given" a new way of helping people.

Not merely the physical act of beautifying someone's nails, but the chance to listen to people and make them feel better about themselves. You don't get the excitement a doctor might feel when a patient is cured, but people do not come into a nail salon to merely look pretty to others, they want to look pretty to themselves.

In essence, you cannot look good to others until you feel good about yourself. An amazing business – people came into my shop feeling rushed, haggard, or consumed by their daily lives and I had been given the joy of letting them walk out feeling great. Yes, it might just be "nails" to some, to others it was a feeling of delight. I was lucky to make them feel this way. Who would have thought (well I guess I did) that the Bishop was right in telling me that I would find numerous ways to help people – ways that might seem small on the outside to others, but not on the inside to the individual.

As the year continued, my business was growing and I was feeling good about myself. In all honesty, I did not give conscious thought that something was missing from my life and, in a way, my personality. I really just didn't "see" it.

I felt a feeling of exuberance when Trach Ba Vu came to visit me that year. His visits just lifted and enlightened me. Here is the "strange" thing; he had a way of reading me that I never could. You really can educate yourself when someone else has the ability to read your inner thoughts.

He suggested that it was time to further "broaden" my life and enjoy a social life. It was time to begin filling that need to begin a family of my own - a family to love, take care of, and grow.

When making a decision of minor importance, I have always found it advantageous to consider all the pros and cons. In vital matters, however, such as the choice of a mate or a profession, the decision should come from the unconscious, from somewhere within ourselves. In the important de-

cisions of personal life, we should be governed, I think, by the deep inner needs of our nature."

Sigmund Freud
(1856 – 1939)

I mentioned to him that the woman of the family I had been living with had this wonderful sister named Thuy (Teresa) who I had known since my first day on that initial visit to Sarasota. I had not really given it any thought throughout the past couple of years, but I did have a fondness for her. Really, I never thought of her as anything but a friend, a person I got to know through family – at least I think I never thought about her in any other way.

"You don't have to go looking for love when it's where you come from."

Werner Erhard
(1935 -)

Trach Ba Vu encouraged (okay, insisted) that I should ask her out for an evening and just enjoy my-self. At least, I "think" that is what he was "thinking" sometimes teachers let you learn on your own.

In true Vietnamese tradition, he accompanied me to Thuy's home and requested from her parents that I might have the privilege of taking Thuy out...I don't know if the word "date" was used. Luckily, they agreed and Thuy and I were to go out for the first of many special evenings.

"Who ever loved that loved not at first sight?"

Christopher Marlowe
(1564 – 1593)

It truly was a magical evening that was followed by many more wonderful dates – yes, they were dates. She provided something special in my life that I never even knew was missing - a feeling of "completeness" that fought off any loneliness and sorrow.

And, Trach Ba Vu knew I needed this and knew it was time. I guess I should be angry – this was one amazing gift that he had that he didn't actually teach me…or, maybe he did.

"One word frees us of all the weight and pain
in life. That word is love."

Sophocles
(496 BC - 406 BC)

It was time once again for Trach Ba Vu to accompany me to the home of Thuy's parents. It was no longer a request for an evening, but for their permission and blessing to marry their daughter.

Their permission delighted me. Thuy's acceptance to my proposal of marriage put me into a state beyond

happiness and excitement. A state or word I don't think I could learn in any dictionary.

A feeling the made both my heart and mind open and grow in unimaginable ways. From all I came from in Vietnam to my progression to being a United States citizen and graduate I was now learning from one of the most powerful forces in God's universe – love.

> *"Neither a lofty degree of intelligence nor*
> *imagination nor both go to the making of genius.*
> *Love, love, love, that is the soul of genius."*
>
> Wolfgang Amadeus Mozart
(1756 – 1791)

Our wedding date was set for January 1, 2003. Thuy and I were married. She helped me fulfill my life and passion to share and be a part of another individual the way that I had always wanted to and the way that Catholic Church helps cultivate – in a very different and even more precious way than I had dreamed possible, even if the Bishop had not.

This was truly a beginning of a new enlightening and wonderful life. Or, maybe I should say the continuation of one that was now taking a new direction fulfilling my goals, my values, and my desire to give and accept love.

In essence, another schoolroom that I was now a part of with yet more amazing gifts being offered to me.

"Love unlocks doors and opens windows that
weren't even there before."

Mignon McLaughlin
(1913 – 1983)

Once again, I was being taught a lesson for which I would be forever grateful. Not a lesson of immediate survival of my being – but the survival and growth of my soul.

"What greater thing is there for two human souls
Than to feel that they are joined together
to strengthen each other in all labour,
To minister to each other in all sorrow,
To share with each other in all gladness,
To be one with each other in the silent
unspoken memories?
I like not only to be loved,
But to be told that I am loved."

George Elliot
(1819 – 1880)

Conclusion

At the age of thirty four, I was a happy, "learned man", a successful businessman, and a loving – and loved - husband. If you "forget" for a moment all of the invaluable things I learned that was given to me inside the school room, I can honestly say my education outside of the schoolroom indeed formed my character and made me the person I am today. And, I don't know how.

In truth, as I look back at these pages, I believe I had no comprehension that I had learned as much as I did…in actuality I had no idea that I was learning things at those different points in my life. It was knowledge that became an inherent part of my nature which continually enabled me to progress forming my dedication and gratitude to schooling and education.

From early responsibility, family values, love, and escaping my homeland in search of opportunity to learning to read and write two languages, becoming a business person, being blessed with an adoptive family, and a loving wife, I have – and continue to be – blessed.

That early feeling of loneliness while staring into the school room and wanting to be "as good" as all of the children inside fueled my obsession to both "fit in" and be better than I was…not even contemplating how fortunate I was at the time.

I wanted to be educated. I wanted to be part of the "in crowd." I wanted to stop feeling sorry for myself because I wasn't like everyone else…which in truth, I wasn't.

"No one can make you feel inferior
without your consent."

Eleanor Roosevelt
(1884 – 1962)

I don't think anyone – including myself – realizes how many important foundations one builds in their life which sets the course for what proceeds. In most cases, foundations that are not even acknowledged at the time set the basis for the future. Often it is not the event that in itself is the foundation, but how you react and what you learn that you either consciously or subconsciously utilize throughout your life.

For many individuals these events are unfortunately horrific. Yet, while the event is negative, the way you react can form your ideals, goals, and ambitions. What you don't want to do ("be") is just as important as what you want to do ("be").

It is definitely not merely the events and reactions that form your foundation, but, also the invaluable lessons you learn from other individuals along your quest – whatever that might be – if in fact, one even knows.

The point is, I knew (again, not entirely consciously) the person I wanted "to be" – which was more important than "what" I wanted "to be." I wanted to learn, find opportunity, grow, help, and love. I was lucky that I took all of the steps to reach (not that it is any way over) my destination.

"He who would fly one day
Must first learn to stand and walk
and run and climb and dance;
One cannot fly into flying."

Friedrich Nietzsche
(1844 – 1900)

At the age of thirty four, I can proudly say I had "turned out" far better than I thought imaginable at the age of five. I was so lucky that I had achieved so much in my life…luck was being given the opportunity – whether it was a thought, a person, or an event. Results took hard work. It is magical when you can see that so many hours, days, and years of hard work (and unforeseen blessings) truly does pay off. I was able to advance toward my dreams – maybe not idealistic to many – miraculous to me.

The thing is, I wasn't done learning and I still needed someone(s) to pass my dreams onto and create a life far beyond my dreams.

In 2005 my son, Matthew Toan, was born.

I am pretty sure I did not learn this word in school, but the only thought that comes to mind is, "Wow!" A son that had provided the definition for the word <u>miracle</u>. The offspring of the love that Thuy and I shared was a being who I was going to share all that I had learned in my past and all that was in the future.

The irony: there were so many lessons I wanted to teach him…there were so many more lessons that he was going to teach me!

I truly wanted my son to have so much "more" than I had in my life – whatever that might be – and I do not mean merely material things. I was going to make sure he took advantage of all of the things that were available to him. The things that were available without hard work. The things that would take work to achieve, with the blessing that he did not have to work for their offering. They were there for him and I wanted my son to surpass me in any and all ways that he could. Most importantly, he was going to have both the love and the education necessary which he deserved, needed, and I was so lucky to provide.

"Many" years ago I struggled for the "luxury" of opportunities and education. I never thought opportunity would prove to be so astronomical.

From the beginning, Thuy and I spent all of the time available to us with Matthew. We treasured in teaching him the simplest things and seeing his amazing smiles. No matter what basics we taught him, he always enjoyed each of his "miraculous achievements."

Of course, walking, talking, and playing were achievements to him. He also had so much fun with learning each word or letter that came his way. I can't lie; I enjoyed his happiness in his early awakening as much as he did.

"Let early education be a sort of amusement;
you will then be better to find out the natural bent."

Plato

(428 BC - 347 BC)
(The Republic, Book VII")

A child wouldn't be considered the "fruits" of education to most, in my case they were. A passion to learn that led me to flee, learn, work, and love. Of course, one could say I am taking liberties with my "simple equation" however, in my case, my initial quest forged me towards the reward of a child.

Matthew was going to be happy, educated, and loved in all ways that were in my power. And, he was not going to be alone.

In 2007 my daughter, Sarah Tram, was born!

Sorry to say it again, but, "Wow!" There was this "princess" in my arms. Sarah, my beautiful and loving daughter was another "student" for me to teach…another professor to teach me.

Many of the most precious and valuable lessons are learned (or given) quite early from a parent. I was fortunate to have had these given to me. As a parent you begin to learn what these lessons were.

> *"Teaching kids to count is fine, but teaching them what counts is best."*
>
> Bob Talbert
> (1936 - 1999)

In reality, my Father never "taught" me love, responsibility, compassion, or respect (to mention a few) they were just things that he bestowed upon me everyday. They became a part of me. Things that I did not need to study, but things that I learned from him and his examples. I do not even know if "learned" is the right word or "received" would be more appropriate.

Although I would tell my children, they would probably not appreciate how lucky they were to automatically be able to go to school. To learn all that the world has to offer them. To realize that the things that come so freely to most like reading and writing were gifts in which to be forever thankful. While I want them to "appreciate" the gift of schooling, I am so happy that to them, it won't be considered a "gift" but. Rather, a "reality." A reality that I hoped they would love…forever.

> *"If there's a single message passed down from each generation of American parents to their children, it is a two-word line: Better yourself, and if there's a temple of self-betterment in each town, it is the local school. We have worshipped there for some time."*
>
> Ellen Goodman
> (1941 -)

It is often said, "That the children are our future." In my case, it was more than true. In my case, I was going to guarantee them (to the best of my abilities) a wonderful future full of love for themselves, for others, and knowledge.

There is so much I have learned and so many people and blessings that I am thankful for helping me to getting me where I am…and so many more lessons, people and blessings that I am thankful for assiting me to getting me to where I am going.

"Conclusion"….I don't think so!

"Know Yourself" — *Socrates*

"Control Yourself" — *Cicero*

"Give Yourself" — *Christ*

Dr. Harold Hyde, President,
New Hampshire Plymouth College
*Accredited as: Surely the shortest
commencement address in history.*

(And the most memorable)

Appendix

"Great Educators"

(This extensive research and diligent compilation was due to the dedicated and professional efforts of Carole Goff.)

Since the beginning of time, there have literally been thousands of individuals who could be considered "Great Educators." These men and women range from authors, playwrights, and philosophers to teachers, statesmen, and of course, society itself.

It would be inconceivable to provide a list of all of these noted contributors to the education of the world… should it be possible to even create such a list.

As such, what follows is a very brief selection of "great minds" with a short synopsis of some of their thoughts.

Socrates (469 – 399 BC)

It is interesting to note that Socrates actually never wrote any of his thoughts down. They were always spoken and subsequently written by others (i.e. Plato) and known as "Socratic Dialogues."

What basically held "them" together was a shared belief that one could reason one's way to the truth by looking and analyzing the "natural causes and effects" of everyday day experiences in order to learn "lessons." Because "they" all disagreed and perceived the same occurrences differently from time to time, "they" deduced that "they" each reached their way to different causes and conclusions and that the natural world contributed its four basic elements of earth, air, fire, and water.

Because "they" "chose" or "agreed to disagree" for the sake of philosophical, they shifted away from natural resources and began to expand the concept of a "way" to teach useful skills to others. This was the actual beginning and onset of the concept to "teaching others to educate them." Subsequently, the Sophosists were the first "Professional Teachers." They went around to the families of young boys to teach them especially "how to argue persuasively" and to teach them "how to make a case" in order to give them ultimate power over their paths and jobs.

This was especially a valuable skill because eventually those boys would, as the heads of households, have to speak in public forums thus, the beginning of the "teachers." In essence, if they could not speak well, their families' fortunes would suffer.

This, then, became the beginning evolution of those who could teach and those who could not as well as the realization that all human beings <u>teach and learn differently</u>.

To sum up a mere few of Socrates' concepts and others' perceptions, the following:

- the innate thirst and curiosity for knowledge

- the first concept of wisdom and knowledge equals power

- some argue that in history many consider there to be only two great educators – one is Socrates and the other is Jesus

- he (Socrates) suggests that true wisdom is the property of the Gods, and that what he has – the human wisdom, this knowledge of his own limitations – is worth hardly anything at all

- he was the first to say that, "it is important to respect education – that it is very important to have education in your life"

- the more educated and experimental man became, the more man's surroundings and tools, and the advancement and development of life progressed.

And, another thousand pages that are not included in this synopsis.

Aristotle – 384 – 322 BC

Again, for simplicity sake, the following are highlights of some of his thoughts and of things he is accredited with:

+ the first tutor and the concept of "tutoring"

+ characterized by Dante as "the master of those who know." He is actually recognized as the best educated individual of his or any other time and his mastery of all the world's knowledge places his name on the list of "Giants of Western thought"

+ began the concept of "logic" and how it pertains to knowledge and thus the wisdom and its lesson learning

+ he studied at Plato's Academy…considered the "first school"

+ he went back to nature (at all levels) and "placed his trust in the careful observation and analysis of nature as our best hope at arriving at the truth" and spent his mature years observing and analyzing a body of knowledge "never before available to one man," and concluded that all things possess an "essence or nature." So that, inside the essence of nature is the potential to be actualized (real) in accordance with that nature i.e. every acorn has the potential to be actualized (real) as a giant oak tree

- after a lifetime of study, Aristotle concluded that every substance, whether found in the natural world or created by "human agency" is unique in that each is striving toward an end consistent with its nature or essence. Each substance (or circumstance) has certain characteristics or performs certain functions that no other substance has or can perform. Unlike the plant or animal world, the defining characteristic of human beings is their ability to ask general questions and to seek answers to them through observation and analysis. In short, human beings are rational animals, questioning and thinking animals capable of philosophical thought

- he was the first to come up with the concept of "happiness" and "virtue" (intellectual and moral)

- he concluded that "happiness" is activity in accordance with virtue – the highest virtue, i.e. "proper virtue will be perfect happiness" and that wisdom is the most "pleasant of virtues"

+ happiness, therefore, must be some form of (thought) contemplation, i.e. if you exercise thought and reason, you are a man of virtue and are therefore, truly happy.

And, another thousand pages that are not included in this synopsis.

Erasmus – 1466 – 1526

+ humanist view of education

+ thought and expression form the twofold material of instruction

+ all knowledge falls into one of two divisions: the knowledge of "truths" and the knowledge of "words"

+ language thus claims the first place in the order of study and learning. Grammar is the most important

+ the right method of acquiring grammar rests upon reading and not upon definitions and rules… "I have no patience with the stupidity of the average teacher of grammar who wastes precious years in hammering rules into children's heads. We need to teach them how to acquire the power of speaking a language."

And, another thousand pages that are not included in this synopsis.

John Locke – 1632 – 1704

+ education is something that adults do to children, the educative process is, at heart, hierarchical, with authority residing in the hands of the adult.

+ education is dependent on the securing of right habits of thought and action, children, especially young children, have not developed enough, intellectually and morally to understand why they must perform certain activities

+ children learn more by example than by mere telling, thus it is crucial to create an environment in which children can learn from the example of their elders

+ the well educating of children is so much the duty and concern of parents

+ as the foundation of this there ought very early on to be imprinted on his mind, a true notion of God as the independent Supreme Being, Author, and Maker of all things, from whom we receive all our good, who loves us, and gives us all things.

And, another thousand pages that are not included in this synopsis.

John Dewey – 1859 – 1952

- considered one of the world's greatest educators

- born the year Horace Mann died

- one of the first to see and read Darwin's *Origin of Species*

- lived through the Civil War and the Great Depression

- first to have and teach the concept of "Social Justice"

- first to establish the "Lab School" as a testing ground for his evolving educational ideas

- founder of coined term "pragmatism"

- published scores of books and hundreds of educational articles

- the first to re-define education based upon experience

- suggested that good experience is characterized by both interaction and continuity and an educational experience is one in which an active mind interacts with a wide open world to solve genuine problems that are continuous with, yet different from, previous experiences

- said that we are creatures of habit, and it is our unique ability to stop, reflect, and then act – to respond intelligently to a problematic situation requiring more than a mere habitual reaction

- all education proceeds by the participation of the individual in the social consciousness of the race, through this unconscious education from birth into early childhood, the individual gradually comes to shame in the intellectual and moral resources which humanity has succeeded in getting together

- the only true education comes through the stimulation of the child's powers by the demands of the social situations in which he finds himself and through these demands he is stimulated to act as a member of a unity, to emerge from his original narrowness of action and feeling, and to conceive of himself from the standpoint of the welfare of the group to which he belongs

- the educational process has two sides – one psychological and one sociological – of the two, the psychological is the basis and the child's own instincts and powers furnish the material and give the starting point for all education – when there is psychological insight and balance, education will flourish, but, without insight into the psychological structure and activities of the individual, the educational process will result in friction and disintegration or arrest the child's nature

- the school is primarily a social institution that is simply that form of community life in which all those agencies are concentrated that will be most effective in bringing the child to share in the resources of society and to use his own powers for social ends

- education, therefore, is a process of living and not a preparation for future living

- the school must represent present life – life as real and vital to the child as that which he carries on in the home, neighborhood, or on the playground

- it should exhibit these activities to the child, and reproduce them in such ways that the child will gradually learn the meaning of them, and be capable of playing his own part in relation to them

- this is a psychological necessity, because it is the only way of securing continuity in the child's growth, the only way of giving a background of past experience to the new ideas given in school

- it is also a social necessity because the home is the form of social life in which the child has been nurtured and in connection with which he has had his moral training and it is the business of the school to deepen and extend his sense of the values bound up in his home life

- much of the present education fails because it neglects this fundamental principle of the school as a form of community life

- the teacher's place and work in the school is to be interpreted from the same basis and the teacher is not in the school to impose certain ideas or to form certain habits in the child but to select the influences which shall affect the child and to assist him in properly responding to these influences

- the image is the great instrument of instruction – what a child gets out of any subject presented to him is simply the images which he himself forms with regard to it

- the child's power of imagery and in seeing to it that he is continually forming definite, vivid, and growing images of the various subjects with which he comes in contact in his experiences

- emotions are the reflex of actions.

And, another thousand pages that are not included in this synopsis.

Horace Mann – 1796 – 1859

- considered to be the great 19th century school reformer

- the main purpose of public education is to develop good character based on religion and moral education should be based on reading the bible

- in this theory, "The Common School" should teach only the pure Republican principles and practices that united Americans in the onset and this is based upon the American History Books that glorified the Founding Fathers

- the creation of the "Common School," with its grass roots governance and consensual curriculum, was one of the triumphs of 19th century reform

- fueled by a powerful Republican ideology and aspiring to create universal education, the "Common School" movement appealed to millennial hope and fear, but, by the turn of the 20th century, reformers grew dissatisfied with local self –rule and a shared curriculum

- once again, the country came to a turning point in the development of it's system of education, as leaders redefined democracy in the new urban and industrial society of the early 20th century

- the start of local control by elected school committees set a democratic stamp on public education, however, rural areas fell short

- a battle ensued – "take the schools out of politics and the politics out of schools"

- reformers wanted to consolidate small rural districts and assert more control of country schools by counties and states

- as the Secretary of Education for the state of Massachusetts, he became a major promoter of public school education and rode his horse from district to district actually reviewing each physical facility

- during his school inspections, he found a system built on inequity - with no state supervision, schools varied widely from town to town

- he visited one thousand schools over the course of six years and wrote detailed reports

- he held public meetings to make changes and proposed a new system of what he called "Common Schools" where they would serve all boys and girls, teach them a common body of knowledge that would give each student an equal chance in life…a free school system

- education then, beyond all other devices of human origin, is the equalizer of the conditions of men, the great balance wheel of the social machinery

- his ideas on school reform made him one of the most influential writers of his time and his victories included state bureaus of education, teacher training, and free tax-supported education

- he has been called "The Patron Saint of Public Education."

And, another thousand pages that are not included in this synopsis.

And, as stated in the beginning, thousands of other Great Educators who have not been included here and who should not be overlooked or under appreciated for their tremendous courage, knowledge, and efforts to the benefit of mankind.

References

Philosophical Documents in Education, Ronald F. Reed and Tony W. Johnson, Longman Publishers USA.

The Collected Dialogues of Plato, Edith Hamilton and Huntington Cairns, Princeton University Press.

The Philosophy of Aristotle, Renford Bambrough, New York: New American Library.

Models of Man: Explorations in the Western Educational Traditions, New York: John Wiley & Sons

Three Thousand Years of Educational Wisdom: Selections from Great Documents, Cambridge, MA: Harvard University Press.

Concerning the Aim and Method of Education, Desiderius Erasmus, translated by William Harrison Woodward, Bureaus of Publications, Classics in Education, Teachers College Press.

Thoughts Concerning Education, John Locke, edited by F.W. Garforth, Oxford, England, Helene Mann Educational Books Ltd.

John Dewey, The Early Works, 1895 – 1898, Jo Ann Boydston, Southern Illinois University Press.

Democracy and Education, John Dewey – Simon and Schuster, 1916, Reprinted with Permission, Copyright 1916 – Macmillan Publishing Company.

Experience and Education. John Dewey (IN: *KAPPA Delta Pi*, 1938), An International Honor Society In Education.

The Republic and the School: Horace Mann on the Education of Free Men, "*Ninth Annual Report*", Edited by Lawrence A. Cremin, New York: Teachers College Press.

"*The School and Society*" *in Dewey on Education,* Edited by Martin Dworkin, New York: Teachers College Press.

Reclaiming a Conversation: The Ideal of the Educational Woman, Jane Roland Martin, Yale University Press.

The School Home: Rethinking Schools for Changing Families, Jane Roland Martin, Cambridge, MASS: Harvard University Press.

Plato Republic Book 7, Translated by Francis Cornford, New York: Oxford University Press.

The Encyclopedia of Philosophy, "*Plato*", Gilbert Ryle, edited by, Paul Edwards, New York: Macmillan.

School, The Story of American Public Education, Sarah Mondale, Sarah B. Patton, Sheila Curran Bernard, edited by Marion Sears Hunter, Beacon Press.